WORLD WAR II

John Perritano

SCHOLASTIC INC. New York Toronto London Auckland Sydney Mexico City New Delhi Hong Kong

Created by Q2AMedia

Editor Jessica Cohn
Publishing Director Chester Fisher
Client Service Manager Santosh Vasudevan
Project Manager Shekhar Kapur
Art Director Sumit Charles
Designer Shipi Sarkar
Art Editor Mariea Janet
Picture Researcher Shreya Sharma

ISBN-13: 978-0-545-17577-7
ISBN-10: 0-545-17577-1

12 11 10 9 8 7 6 5 4 3 2   9 10 11 12 13 14/0

Printed in the U.S.A.   40

First Scholastic printing, September 2009

CONTENT

PATH TO WAR

World War I (1914–1918) took the lives of millions of people. Blood flowed in Europe for a long time, and empires fell. Some nations disappeared. New countries rose from the remains.

German tanks rolled through Libya when the fighting began in North Africa.

ALLIES EMERGE

World War I, the "War to End All Wars," ended in 1918. Many people hoped for lasting peace. Yet, the First World War sowed the seeds for an even greater conflict—the Second World War. In World War II, Germany, Italy, and Japan fought the Allied powers. The Allied powers included Great Britain, the Soviet Union, and the United States. WWII involved most of the world's nations.

UNITED NATIONS

After the war, the Allies set up the United Nations (UN) to try to settle quarrels between countries and avoid future wars. World War II had forced the United States to end its **isolationism**. Members of the UN hoped that they had learned the lessons of WWII.

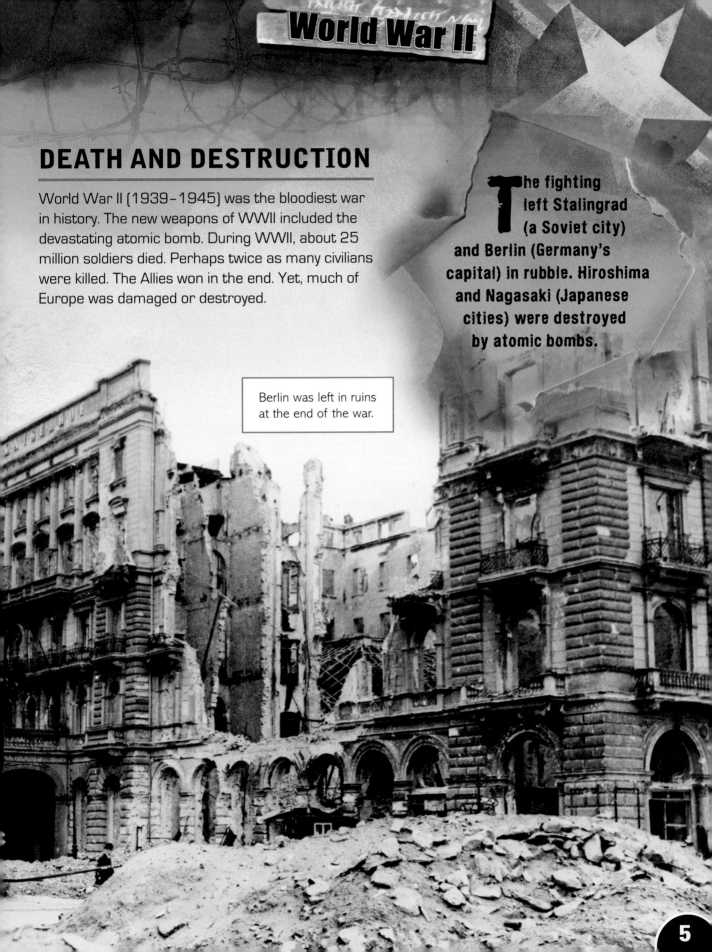

DEATH AND DESTRUCTION

World War II (1939–1945) was the bloodiest war in history. The new weapons of WWII included the devastating atomic bomb. During WWII, about 25 million soldiers died. Perhaps twice as many civilians were killed. The Allies won in the end. Yet, much of Europe was damaged or destroyed.

The fighting left Stalingrad (a Soviet city) and Berlin (Germany's capital) in rubble. Hiroshima and Nagasaki (Japanese cities) were destroyed by atomic bombs.

Berlin was left in ruins at the end of the war.

VERSAILLES

The Second World War began only about 20 years after the end of the First World War. How could the world fight another bloody war so soon? Part of the answer has to do with the Treaty of Versailles, the peace agreement that ended World War I in 1918.

TREATY OF VERSAILLES

The treaty got its name because officials from the warring nations met in Versailles, France. Most officials who signed the treaty wanted to produce a lasting peace. Many Allied leaders, however, also wanted revenge against Germany. They wanted to punish the Germans.

THE PAYBACK

The Treaty of Versailles gutted Germany's military. It forced the Germans to pay billions of dollars in **reparations** to the Allied nations for war damages. "This is not peace. It is an **armistice** for 20 years," predicted French commander Marshal Ferdinand Foch.

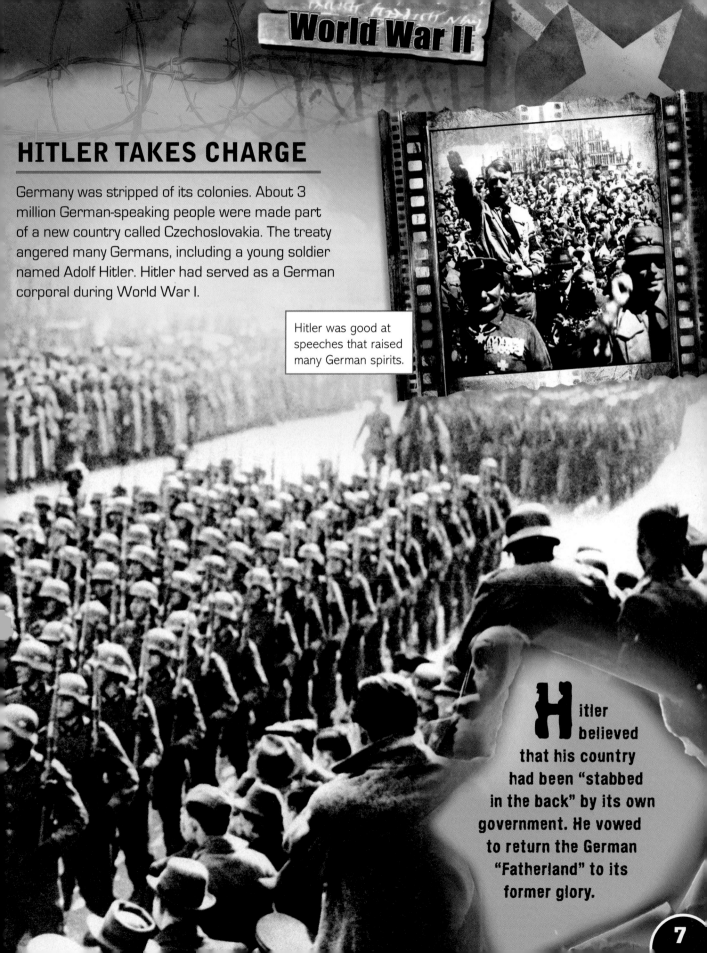

HITLER TAKES CHARGE

Germany was stripped of its colonies. About 3 million German-speaking people were made part of a new country called Czechoslovakia. The treaty angered many Germans, including a young soldier named Adolf Hitler. Hitler had served as a German corporal during World War I.

Hitler was good at speeches that raised many German spirits.

Hitler believed that his country had been "stabbed in the back" by its own government. He vowed to return the German "Fatherland" to its former glory.

NEW EMPIRES

Born in Austria in 1889, Hitler was the son of a customs official. Hitler dropped out of high school when he was 16. In 1920, he formed the National Socialist German Workers' Party, which became known as the Nazi Party. In 1923, Hitler attempted to overthrow the German government.

HITLER'S RISE

Hitler's plot failed, and he was arrested. While in prison Hitler wrote a book he titled *Mein Kampf*, or *My Struggle*, which laid out his plans for the future. After a year behind bars, Hitler was freed and began rebuilding the Nazi Party. By the 1930s, Germany's money was worthless. Millions of Germans did not have jobs. They cried for change. Hitler's speeches inspired the nation. He quickly rose to power.

Nazi party members held rallies to gain support from the people.

PLACING BLAME

Hitler blamed Jews and communists for Germany's problems. He declared that the "Aryan race" was special. Who was Aryan? The Nazis considered white people of Northern European heritage to be Aryans. Hitler declared the Nazis the only political party. The government passed **repressive** laws against Jews.

CHANGE IN MANY LANDS

The Nazis won seats in the German parliament. In 1933, Hitler became Germany's chancellor. Soon the iron fist of Hitler came smashing down. He stripped Germany's state governments of their powers. Meanwhile, **fascist** governments also were taking hold in Italy and Spain. The military was taking over in Japan. Italy and Japan took steps to create their own empires. They built up their armies.

Benito Mussolini took charge in Italy.

In 1931, Japan invaded the Chinese province of Manchuria, hoping to create an empire. Four years later, Italy invaded the African nation of Ethiopia. Italy's leader, Benito Mussolini, wanted an empire like the former Roman Empire.

GERMANY RISING

Adolf Hitler ignored the rules of the Treaty of Versailles. He worked to rebuild Germany's military. He killed or imprisoned anyone who opposed him. The German leader made friends with Mussolini. Germany and Italy formed the Rome-Berlin Axis. The Axis powers would later include Japan.

A GATHERING STORM

In 1938, Hitler invaded Austria, Germany's neighbor. He succeeded in merging Austria with Germany. The German leader also wanted to rule the Sudetenland, an area in Czechoslovakia where German was spoken. Neville Chamberlain, the British prime minister, knew about Hitler's plans. Chamberlain feared a deadly repeat of World War I. He looked for a **compromise** in order to avoid another war.

BROKERING PEACE

Great Britain's Prime Minister Chamberlain went to Germany to meet with Hitler in 1938. Chamberlain wasn't trying to help Hitler; the British leader believed he was avoiding war. British and German officials tried to reach agreement on the future of the Sudetenland. Chamberlain returned home, declaring that he had achieved "peace in our time."

Neville Chamberlain, Britain's prime minister, met with Hitler to try to avoid combat.

APPEASEMENT

In September 1938, Britain and France gave Czechoslovakia a message. Neither major power would stop Germany if Hitler took over the Sudetenland. That policy, known as **appeasement**, only made Hitler bolder. Hitler's troops marched into Bohemia, Moravia, and Slovakia. Poland seemed to be next on his list of targets.

The German army was trained to conquer Europe and create an empire.

By the end of March 1939, the British and French were fed up. They vowed to defend Poland if the Nazis attacked. Europe once again appeared to be heading toward war.

BLITZKRIEG

In the summer of 1939, the people of Poland feared German invasion. The Poles were tough fighters with an army of 1 million. Yet, they were no match for the mighty German war machine. Polish leaders decided that, should Germany attack, they would fight back as long as possible, hoping that Britain and France would come to the rescue.

Germany sent heavy artillery into Poland.

LIGHTNING WAR

The Poles did not, however, expect what happened next. During the early morning hours of September 1, 1939, in a surprise attack, German war machines swept into Poland by air and by land. The Germans called it "blitzkrieg," or lightning war. Germany headed across the Polish border with more than 2,000 tanks and 1,000 planes. The Germans smashed Poland's defenses. Germany's air force, the Luftwaffe, destroyed much of Poland's air force while many of its planes were still on the ground.

HELP FROM THE SOVIETS

Poland surrendered on September 28, 1939. The Soviet Union secretly had formed an **alliance** with Germany before the invasion. Each side agreed not to attack the other. Soviet troops took over the eastern part of Poland, imprisoning thousands of people, including Polish soldiers.

THE WAR MACHINE

Britain and France declared war on Germany on September 3. Unfortunately, neither country was in any position to face down the Nazi **juggernaut**. Britain did not have enough troops. Yet, British aircraft went after German combat forces as the Germans advanced through the Polish countryside. The French made plans to defend their homeland, based on their Maginot Line, defensive fortifications they had built on France's eastern border with Germany.

With Poland in Nazi hands, Hitler spoke of peace with the Allies. But he did not really want to settle differences with Britain and France. He just wanted time for his army to rest and gain strength. Hitler planned to march next against Belgium, Holland, and France. His peace offering gave the nations a false sense of security.

NAZI ADVANCE

As the Nazis turned their attention to Western Europe, the British sent a small defensive force there to slow down the Germans. In April 1940, Germany invaded Denmark and Norway. In May, the Germans quickly conquered Belgium, the Netherlands, and Luxembourg.

When Paris fell, many Parisians could not contain their grief.

ONWARD MARCH

Germany raced toward the English Channel. The Germans successfully cut through the middle of the British and French forces. Winston Churchill, Britain's new prime minister, tried to control the situation. By late May, however, the Germans had trapped the Allied forces near Dunkirk, a port in northern France.

AT DUNKIRK

When the Germans trapped the Allies in Dunkirk, rescue ships urgently set sail to Dunkirk from Britain and other parts of France. Many Allied troops were rescued. However, the road to Paris, the capital of France, now was open.

FALL OF FRANCE

The Nazis began their successful invasion of France on June 5. On June 14, German troops marched into Paris. That same morning, the Nazi flag was hung beneath a great arch in Paris. Many French openly wept at the sight. France signed a surrender agreement with the Nazis on June 22.

French officials signed the papers in the same railway car that Germany had signed the Versailles Treaty that ended World War I. When France fell, Great Britain stood alone against the Axis juggernaut.

The Allies sent rescue ships to Dunkirk, a seaport on the coast of France.

BATTLE OF BRITAIN

Hitler hated the British. He began plans to invade their island nation. Hitler, however, first wanted to make sure his forces controlled the air. Then they could start a successful invasion by sea. The air attack, today known as the Battle of Britain, began in July 1940.

AGAINST ENGLAND

German aircraft heavily bombed British factories and airfields. In August, more than a thousand German planes were attacking each day. Hitler then ordered bombing to begin on English cities, including London. British fighter pilots fought back. By mid-September, the Germans had lost more than a thousand planes and thousands of crew members.

German bombers filled the skies over London.

HOLDING OFF THE TIDE

Britain's brave defense forced Hitler to delay his invasion. Ernie Pyle was an American newspaper reporter based in London. He reported how well the British people endured the German bombing. "It isn't flag-waving... . It is simply a quaint old British idea that nobody is going to push them around." President Roosevelt pushed the United States to give Britain 50 old destroyers. In return, Britain gave the United States some military bases in the Caribbean and Canada. The U.S. Congress passed the Lend-Lease Act, which provided Great Britain with military supplies. Great Britain agreed to repay America after the war.

On June 22, 1941, Germany broke its pact with the Soviet Union. About 3 million German soldiers attacked the Soviets. The Germans used 4,000 tanks, 7,000 pieces of artillery, and 3,000 aircraft. The Soviets and Germans fought each other for the next four long years.

AMERICA WATCHES

Americans watched the growing war with concern. U.S. isolationists spoke out. They wanted the U.S. government to stay out of the war. The United States had long been suffering economic troubles known as the Depression and was officially **neutral**. Yet, President Franklin Roosevelt could see that Great Britain needed America's help to survive.

Hitler attacked Great Britain's cities with all his might.

AMERICA AT WAR

In the Pacific, the Japanese were on the march. In 1940, Japan joined Italy and Germany as part of the Axis alliance. In July 1941, Japan invaded French Indochina. The United States stopped sending oil to Japan in response.

ATTACK ON PEARL HARBOR

Japanese and U.S. officials met to discuss peaceful solutions. Yet, Japanese Admiral Isoroku Yamamoto had a secret plan to destroy the U.S. fleet based in Pearl Harbor, Hawaii. Yamamoto launched his surprise attack against U.S. forces on December 7, 1941, at 7:55 A.M. The Japanese unleashed 353 airplanes from six aircraft carriers. Bombs and torpedoes rained down on the unsuspecting U.S. fleet.

DESTRUCTION AND DECLARATION

Five torpedoes ripped through the side of the battleship USS *Oklahoma*. Hundreds of sailors were trapped belowdecks. The battleship *Arizona* blew up and sunk in the harbor, killing 1,177 Americans on board. More than 2,300 Americans were killed that day. The next day, Roosevelt went before Congress. The president asked for a declaration of war. "The American people in their righteous might will win through to absolute victory," said Roosevelt.

"THIS IS NO DRILL"

On December 7, in Washington, D.C., a ringing telephone interrupted President Franklin Roosevelt, who was speaking with his military adviser Harry Hopkins. Secretary of the Navy Frank Knox was on the line. Knox told the president that he had received an urgent message from Pearl Harbor. The message said: "AIR RAID PEARL HARBOR ... This is no drill."

An anxious nation listened to their radios. Congress declared war against Japan the following day. Germany declared war on the United States on December 11. On December 12, the United States went to war against Germany and Italy.

World War II

The bombing of Pearl Harbor pulled the United States into the war.

SLEEPING GIANT

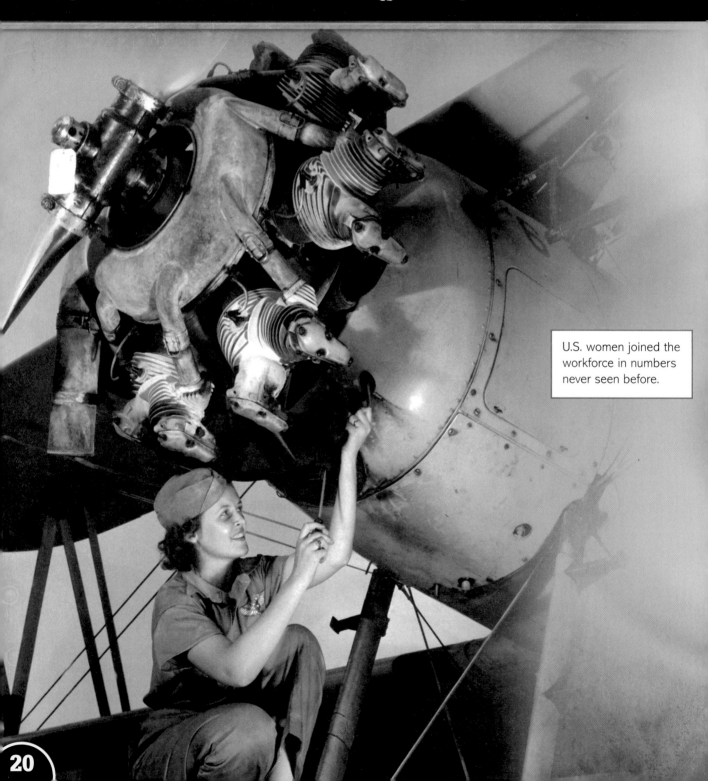

U.S. women joined the workforce in numbers never seen before.

In response to Pearl Harbor, thousands of Americans joined the armed forces. The rest of America quickly got to work. Factories that had once made cars started producing tanks. School children collected scrap metal for America's factories. Women went to work to support the war effort. They made guns, bombs, tanks, and battleships.

WIDENING WAR

While Americans **rationed** gas and **mobilized** in other ways, the war widened. In 1942, the Soviets were battling the Nazis alone on Europe's eastern front. The Soviets desperately wanted the United States and Britain to open a second front against Germany in the west. After much discussion, the United States and Great Britain instead attacked the Germans in occupied French North Africa.

OPERATION TORCH

The Allied plan worked, though not immediately. The Allies fought to push the Axis out of North Africa, to gain control of the Mediterranean Sea. The Allies fought the Germans and Italians in Africa.

U.S. soldiers marched across Italy.

The Allies surprised the Germans by invading Algeria and Morocco in November 1942. Deaths mounted quickly. The Americans were not yet prepared for battling the seasoned Axis soldiers. Yet, the Americans soon learned how to fight as an army. By May 1943, the Allies forced the Axis to retreat out of Africa. Sicily and the Italian mainland were to be invaded next. Allied victory happened fast on the Italian island of Sicily. But fighting in the rest of Italy was long and hard. The winter of 1943–1944 was the worst in years. Cold and mud slowed the Allied advance to Rome. The great city finally fell on June 4, 1944. The Allies had gained an important foothold in southern Europe.

IN THE PACIFIC

While fighting raged in Africa and Italy, the war in the Pacific was also heating up. Guam, New Guinea, the Solomon Islands, and the Philippines had fallen to the Japanese.

IN THE PHILIPPINES

The loss of the Philippines was the most discouraging for the Americans. American and Filipino forces were sick and hungry. They defended the Philippine Islands as best they could, but finally had to surrender on April 9, 1942. The Japanese captured almost 78,000 Allied troops. The Japanese forced their prisoners to march to a prison camp. Many U.S. soldiers died during the march.

Japanese troops fought in the Battle of Guadalcanal, which lasted from August 1942 to February 1943.

ISLAND HOPPING

U.S. General Douglas MacArthur and Admiral Chester Nimitz came up with a plan to beat the Japanese called "island hopping." The **strategy** called for American troops to attack and occupy one island after another across the Pacific all the way to Japan. The Americans hit the enemy at its weakest points. Using this strategy, the Americans won decisive battles at Guadalcanal, Tarawa, and other islands.

MIDWAY ISLAND

The Japanese took aim at Midway Island, a tiny atoll in the Pacific about 1,000 miles northwest of Hawaii. The Japanese wanted to destroy the island's defenses and force American aircraft carriers out into the open. Instead, Midway marked the beginning of the end for the Japanese in the Pacific. The Americans broke a secret Japanese code and discovered their plan. The United States attacked Japan's fleet first.

After Midway Island, the Japanese navy would never recover. From that point on, America was on the offense in the Pacific.

The Battle of Midway ended well for the Americans.

ON TO BERLIN

Hitler believed that after five years of fighting, Germany still could defeat the Allies. Yet, the Soviets continued to press from the east. The Allies came at the German forces in Italy and prepared to invade Western Europe through France.

D-DAY

The Allied invasion of Europe that began on June 6, 1944, was called D-Day. Allied planners had secretly assembled the greatest naval invasion force ever. In a risky crossing of the English Channel, Allied troops headed for the beaches of Normandy, France. It was an unexpected place to attack. Hitler believed it was a **diversion**. He thought the main invasion would come elsewhere. Within days, thousands of Allied forces were moving across France. By late 1944, the Allies were marching across Belgium.

D-Day was the start of the Allied trek across German-occupied lands.

D-DAY NUMBERS

By nightfall of the first day of the main Allied invasion, more than 130,000 troops were ashore. Although Allied casualties were high, they had successfully begun Europe's **liberation**. Eventually more than 2,800,000 Allied soldiers, sailors, and airmen would be in Europe.

On D-Day, Allied troops unloaded the supplies they would need from huge carriers.

BATTLE OF THE BULGE

Then Hitler ordered a surprise counterattack. He used 1,000 tanks and other military might. Germans charged through the snow-covered Ardennes Forest. The Germans pushed back a section of the Allied front lines. The Battle of the Bulge had begun. The shocked Allies retreated but did not surrender. The weather was freezing cold. Bad weather grounded the Allied planes. The counterattack seemed to be working for the Germans. Then the Germans encountered trouble, too. Some of their tanks ran out of gas.

By late January 1945, the Germans retreated. More than 100,000 Germans died or were wounded. Allied casualties totaled 80,000. It was the last of the Germans' great offensives.

END IN EUROPE

The British and Americans pressed westward. The Soviets moved eastward. The end of the war was in sight. U.S. President Franklin Roosevelt, British Prime Minister Winston Churchill, and Soviet leader Joseph Stalin met to decide Germany's postwar fate.

GIs fought their way into German-held territory.

IN YALTA

The Allied leaders met at Yalta and made a plan to divide Germany into occupied zones. The Soviets, British, Americans, and French would each control one zone after the war. At the same meeting, the Soviets agreed to enter the war against Japan in the Pacific.

SURRENDER!

As Allied soldiers moved into Nazi-held areas of Europe, they discovered Nazi death camps. The Nazis had murdered between 9 to 11 million innocent people. Allied troops liberated the few surviving camp prisoners.

On April 30, 1945, Hitler, his wife, and several other Nazi leaders killed themselves before they could be captured in a secret Berlin bunker. Soon after, the German general left in charge surrendered to the Allies. The terrible war in Europe was over.

THE FINAL SOLUTION

Inside the Nazi death camps, millions of Jews and others had been put to death. The killings were part of Hitler's plan known as the "Final Solution." The names of the camps—Buchenwald, Auschwitz, Dachau, and others—would become infamous.

The survivors of the death camps told stories of inhumane horrors.

THE ATOMIC BOMB

President Roosevelt did not live to see Hitler's defeat. Roosevelt had died suddenly on April 15, 1945. Former Vice President Harry S. Truman was the new U.S. president. He took charge of the war against Japan, which continued even after Germany's surrender.

FORCING SURRENDER

On August 6, 1945, a U.S. B-29 bomber dropped the first atomic bomb on Hiroshima, Japan. A mushroom cloud of smoke rose above the city. About 70,000 people were killed immediately. Three days later, the Americans dropped a second bomb, on Nagasaki, Japan. On August 14, Emperor Hirohito announced Japan's unconditional surrender.

A mushroom-shaped cloud rose over Hiroshima.

THE ATOMIC BOMBS

When Truman came to office, American scientists in New Mexico had already tested the world's first atomic bomb. The test bomb had never-before-seen destructive power. The U.S. scientists then prepared two atomic bombs that could be used against enemies. The scientists nicknamed the two bombs Fat Man and Little Boy.

END OF THE WAR

The end formally came on September 2, 1945. The Japanese minister of foreign affairs signed papers of surrender. The greatest conflict in human history was finally over.

A new world order arose. The United States emerged from World War II more powerful than it ever had been, the world's first superpower. Unfortunately, some friends became **adversaries**. An **ideological** struggle arose between former allies the United States and the Soviet Union. This struggle became known as the Cold War. Yet, other former enemies became friends.

The United States helped rebuild a devastated Europe (including Germany) and Japan. Today, the influences of World War II still affect the nations of the world, which try to learn from its lessons.

The papers of surrender were signed aboard the USS *Missouri*.

GLOSSARY

adversaries—opponents or enemies

alliance—a group that forms to help one another

appeasement—an attempt to maintain peace by giving in to someone

armistice—when war is stopped by agreement

compromise—a settlement for which each side gives up something

destroyers—small, fast warships

diversion—a plan used to distract an enemy from a real attack

fascist—a political philosophy of total control, usually under a dictator

ideological—relating to a set of beliefs of a particular individual or group

isolationism—holding back from political or economic relations with other countries

juggernaut—a force too powerful to stop

liberation—freedom

mobilized—assembled and made ready, as if for war

neutral—not wanting to take part in something, as in a war between countries

rationed—used in controlled amounts, often for purposes of conserving resources

reparations—payments used to repair a past harm

repressive—causing something or someone to be held back

strategy—a military plan

SOURCES

Books

The American Story World War II. Sarah Brash. Time–Life, 1997.

Causes and Consequences of World War II. Stewart Ross. Steck Vaughn Company, 1996.

The Second World War A Complete History. Martin Gilbert. Holt and Company, 1989.

The Second World War. John Keegan. Penguin, 1989.

A Short History of World War II. James L. Stokesbury. William Morrow & Company, Inc.

The War in the Desert. Richard Collier. Time-Life, 1977.

Web

http://www.bbc.co.uk/history/worldwars/wwtwo/

http://www.grolier.com/wwii/wwii_mainpage.html

http://www.worldwar-2.net/

INDEX

WORLD WAR II

World War II (1939–1945) was the "Big One"—a global conflict involving most of the world's nations. Brutal fighting was waged across the globe. Millions died as the Axis and Allied powers fought to control the future of the world. See why . . . inside.

Learn more!

Each book in the America at War series comes with a CD-ROM with many interactive features.

ISBN-13: 978-0-545-17577
ISBN-10: 0-545-17577-1

EAN

9 780545 175777